To my mom
Helen Eberhart Daley
and all those memories of angelic Christmases.

DDM

To
Taylor
your humble, yet radiant Christmas spirit—
a blessing like His in disguise.

SWC

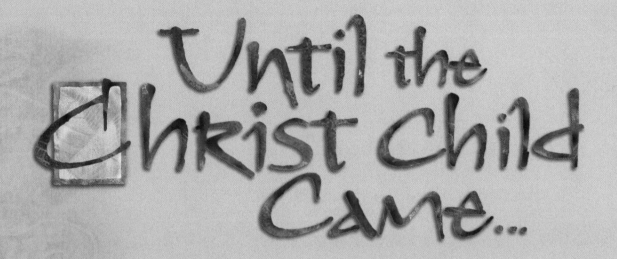

Until the Christ Child Came...

WRITTEN BY

DANDI DALEY MACKALL

ILLUSTRATED BY

SALLY WERN COMPORT

CONCORDIA PUBLISHING HOUSE

Mary loved the carpenter.

She dreamt of Joseph's honest face,

And canopies and wedding lace;

And everything was all in place...

...Until the angel came.

The angel came to Mary's room

In whistling wind and shimmering wings,

And whispering such amazing things:

"You'll bear God's Son, the King of kings!"

She thought, what wondrous news he brings!

...Until she wondered how.

"How can it be? I'm not a bride.

What miracle has God designed?"

Had any man or womankind

Been asked to leave so much behind?

Said yes like that, with soul and mind...

...Until she said, "I will."

She said, "I will," and bowed in prayer,

As peace and joy replaced her fright.

She thought of Joseph in the night,

Believed that all would work out right...

...Until the word got out.

The word got out. "A virgin birth?"

They called her names. They said she lied.

It broke her heart when Joseph cried.

She passed her days in quiet pride...

...Until her Joseph came.

Her Joseph came. He'd had a dream.

His face still shone with angel glow.

"This child was sent by God—I know!"

He took her hand and squeezed it so;

She thought her love might overflow...

...Until the message came.

The message came from Caesar's hand.

A tax demand, a world decree:

Each man must pay a royal fee,

Be counted with his family.

So Joseph left from Galilee...

...'Til Mary said, "I'll come."

"I'll come with you to Bethlehem."

She felt the child within her leap.

And though the way was hard and steep,

They journeyed on, their spirits deep...

...Until they reached the town.

They reached the town of Bethlehem

That teemed with travelers in retreat.

No room, no bed, no food to eat.

And Joseph's words grew bittersweet:

"She'll have the baby in the street!"

...Until they found the barn.

An old innkeeper had a barn.

"It's nothing but a stable bare,

But you could have your baby there."

And Joseph gently stroked her hair...

...Until the pain began.

She hadn't counted on the pain.

Could blessings ever hurt so much?

No doctor, midwife, mother's touch—

Her faith was all she found to clutch...

...Until she heard the cry.

She heard the cry—her baby born!

And Joseph laughed; then Joseph wept.

While Mary nursed, the baby slept.

The shepherds came as daylight crept...

...Until the morning dawned.

Mary loved the Carpenter.

She touched His face and called His name.

Heard wise men speak of Jesus' fame,

The hope of all the poor and lame,

Knew things would never be the same...

...Until the end of time.

SAINT LOUIS

Text copyright © 2002 Dandi Daley Mackall

Illustrations copyright © 2002 Sally Wern Comport

Published by Concordia Publishing House

3558 S. Jefferson Avenue, St. Louis, MO 63118-3968

Manufactured in China

1   2   3   4   5   6   7   8   9   10   11   10   09   08   07   06   05   04   03   02